The HOW TO MAKE GOOD STUFF HAPPEN PLAY-WORK-BOOK
©2006, Deborah Ivanoff and Abigail Ivanoff-Achenbach,
An Introduction to
BEING THE SOLUTION by Darel Rutherford
All Rights Reserved www.richbits.com

Warning Disclaimer
This book is designed to provide information in regard to the subject matter covered. It is sold with the understanding that the publisher and author are not engaged in rendering legal, accounting or other professional services. If legal or other expert assistance is required, the services of a competent professional should be sought. The purpose of this book is to educate and entertain. The Author and DAR Publishing shall have neither liability nor responsibility to any person or entity with respect to any loss or damage, caused or alleged to be caused, directly or indirectly by the information contained in this book.

If you do not wish to be bound by the above, you may return this book to the publisher for a full refund.

Published by
DAR Publishing
7116 Arroyo Del Oso NE
Albuquerque, NM 87109

All rights reserved. No part of this book may be reproduced, transmitted in any form or by any means, electronic or mechanical, including photocopying, recording, or by any information storage and retrieval system without permission in writing from the authors, except for inclusion of brief quotations in a review, in which case full credit must be given.

Copyright October 2006 by Deborah Ivanoff and Abigail Ivanoff-Achenbach
Printed in the United States of America

Table of Contents

Part One, Getting Started 7
1. Gratitude 10
2. Law of Attraction 12
3. Life is a Game 15
4. Your Traveling Companions 19
5. We All Live In a Box 24

PART TWO, The Creating Process 28
6. Why Do You Want It? 29
7. Believing Is Seeing 33
8. BE DO HAVE 36
9. Magnetic Formula For Momentum 39
10. First Believe Then Take Action 46
11. The Gap 51
12. How Do You Know When It's Working? 55
13. The Power Pause 61
14. Powerpacts 65
15. Gratitude 68
16. What Now? 71

Contact Us 72

Thank you for purchasing HOW TO MAKE GOOD STUFF HAPPEN, the PLAY-WORK-BOOK for KIDS (and Their Adults) **based on the teachings of Darel Rutherford in BEING THE SOLUTION.**

November 2004

This book wrote itself. You might think I'm kidding, but "the book" literally "woke me up" from a Sunday morning, only-day-to-sleep-in-late-deep-sleep; at 5 am in the monring, no less!

I was excited to answer Inspiration's call. None-the-less, I attempted to make a few notes and return to the comfort of warm quilts against a cold Fall morning.

But my Muse would have none of that. This book began "writing itself" in my head and finally I gave in to it's insistence. Armed with fluffy slippers and hot tea, I spread myself out over my living room table and couch, and proceeded to outline the book in its entirety in less than an hour and a half.

Creating the finished product took a bit longer, but was great fun as my partner in this project has been my beloved daughter, Abigail.

To complete this book and bring it to you, we used the very same processes that are outlined in the book, BEING THE SOLUTION, by Darel Rutherford.

I have had the unique benefit of learning and working with Darel Rutherford for over 6 years. This book is the direct result of his personal mentoring and teachings from BEING THE SOLUTION, applied and practiced diligently in my life and in the life of my family. Every child and adult can benefit from using these tools as each of us travels our paths of growh, empowerment and BECOMING our most glorious selves.

May this PLAYbook serve you and your family, friends and associates well. In Joy!

Deborah Ivanoff

June 2005

When my mom first told me about the idea of the book I thought it might be a little odd that I, as an eleven-year-old could be writing a book.

I thought that is was cool that I was able to write this book with my mom. She does such great work with other people that I wanted to do something great with her.

Abigail Ivanoff-Achenbach

A Special Thank You

A special thank you again to Darel Rutherford, who has been inspiration, coach, advocate and friend (and the occassional diplomatic mediator for my own "angel" and "beastie", see Chapter 4). His work changed, and continues to change, my life, and my family's life, in ways that are bigger, bolder, and better. I am honored to have the opportunity to explore the BEING solution within myself and support it's practice in others' lives through the classes, coaching and mentoring programs we have co-created.

Thanks too, to Carolyn Wilson-Elliott and Sherry Hudson, coaches and mentors of mine. Thanks to Quantum Spirit International, and its exceptional coach training program, Spiritual Cross Training, which trains coaches to BE in their own process so they may sit in confidence of their clients power of choice as the client discovers his/her own inspired solutions.

Thanks to Sherry Jamarillo for all the many, many ways she keeps BEING THE SOLUTION Central flowing smoothly. She too, exemplifies Darel's profound work. And I have relished our friendship. Everyone should get the chance to have this much fun and satisfaction at work.

And finally, but not least, thank you to both my incredible children, Abigail and Isaac; my most challenging and valued teachers. BEing your mom has been the greatest gift the Universe could give me. I look forward to many wonderful years sharing the joys and delights of this world of our own design.

Deborah

PART ONE

GETTING STARTED

On BEING and BEcoming

Remember a time you wanted to do something. Maybe you wanted to clean your room but you just didn't feel like doing it. Or maybe you wanted to play the guitar like your favorite band member but you just couldn't bring yourself to practice.

Well, if you NEVER did do what it takes to complete the task or acquire the skill, then you have an ideal memory of what happens when you make a BEING choice. You chose to be the one who did not follow through.

And if you DID do what it takes to clean the room or learn the instrument, what changed? It wasn't something on the outside that changed you (although you may have had certain incentives delivered via parents, boss, etc).

Right, it was YOU who changed WHO you were BEING. One moment you were the person who didn't practice and something in you shifted and then you practiced..

It all starts with a BEING choice. And that's what this book is all about; making changes in your life from the correct starting point and then following through in ways that Make More Good Stuff Happen, more easily, with full awareness of what's happening and how to repeat this process.

Law of Attraction

Most people agree that on Earth, what goes up must come down. When you toss a ball into the air, you expect it to fall down to Earth again.

Most of us agree, gravity is a natural law, at work here on planet earth.

A universal law is something that can never be broken, it works the same way every time.

There is a law in our universe that we can observe when we watch for it. Whatever we think about, we pull to us, just like a powerful magnet.

When we think about how great everything is, more great stuff shows up. And when we're convinced we woke up on the wrong side of the bed; sure enough, things don't go so well.

That's the Law of Attraction working it's magic!

Chapter 1

Gratitude

Most people begin wanting something by wishing for it. Then they notice they don't have it. The more they notice they don't have it with the accompanying FEELINGS of LACK the farther they push it from them. To make matters worse, they often hold the picture in their mind of what-they-want-but-don't-have, so they actually ATTRACT "not having it".

That's why we begin our process of "making more good stuff happen" by thinking about all the "stuff" we are already thankful for.

As we remember how wonderful the "good stuff" is NOW and really FEEL that; how wonderful the "good stuff is now", our "attraction magnet" gets stronger, and stronger, and stronger.

Then with our SUPERCHARGED Attraction Magnet we think of what we DO want and our GOOD FEELINGS start to pull it our way.

What Can You Feel Good About Now?

Think for a moment about all the things and people and pets and places you are thankful for. Write some down here so you can remember them each day. Before you think about what you want, think about WHAT YOU HAVE and let yourself FEEL really, really happy and thankful about it.

_____

_____

_____

_____

_____

_____

_____

_____

Chapter 2

Law of Attraction

What happens when you tune your radio to a Country Western station? Do you hear Country Western music?

And when you tune to the Rock-and-Roll station, do you hear Rock-and-Roll?

You wouldn't expect to hear Country Western on the Rock-and-Roll station, would you?

Well, if you want something, say a new friend, but you "stay tuned" to the "station" in your mind that plays the song "I wish I had a friend, I don't have a friend, everyone else has friends"...are you going to hear and see a new friend? No, of course not!

In order to attract that new friend, you must "tune in" to the "station" in your mind that plays the song "I'm a good friend, I love having friends, I'm excited about meeting new friends."

So STAY TUNED to what you DO want to see, feel and have in your life so that "station", and only that "station", plays for you.

Abigail's Story

I Want a Pony!

When my friend, Brinn and I first came across a book about miniature horses, I thought, "they're so cute" and we checked out a book about miniature horses from the library. Then I started reading about them. Yes, they were cute but they're also a lot of responsibility.

We checked out many more books and our desire for a miniature horse grew. We both discussed the possibility of buying a miniature horse with our mothers' help and keeping them in the field next door.

My mother said that I could have a miniature horse, if she didn't have to pay for it, or clean up after it. She encouraged my friend and I to keep visualizing our miniature horse and stay open to possibilities that we couldn't yet imagine.

What a surprise it was, when our neighbor, who had 12 horses already, called us to come visit her.....you guessed it....new miniature horses! Not one, but three miniature horses had just arrived!

She told Brinn and I we could come visit and play with the three miniature horses anytime we wanted.

Tune In, Turn Up the Volume of What You Want

What do you want right now? Write, or draw a picture of that, or a symbol that stands for it, on the line below.

1. What do you want? _____

Imagine you had a dial that could magically "tune in or tune out" that thing, and turn the volume "up or down". What is the radio station in your mind playing right now? Listen and write it down below.

2. What is "playing in your mind"? _____

Is that what you want to listen to? Will it ATTRACT to you what you want (what you wrote on line 1)?

If "playing" those thoughts, feelings and actions won't bring what you DO want, imagine that with that "magic dial" you slowly but surely "turn those thoughts down" that won't bring you what you are wanting.

So, what are the thoughts, feelings and actions you want to "tune in to"? Write those below.

3. List the thoughts, feelings and actions that you DO want to listen to _____

_____

Now, with that "magic dial", tuned into the correct station for what you are wanting, TURN THE VOLUME UP slowly but surely. Do that now. Turn UP the volume of the thoughts, feelings and actions that you DO WANT. Wow, doesn't it FEEL good to "listen" to what you DO want as you imagine it in your mind?

Chapter 3

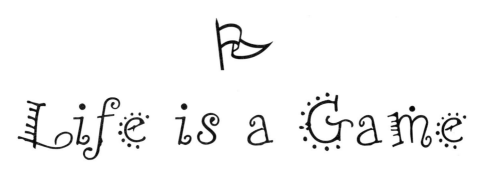

Life is a Game

Maybe you've heard the phrase "Life is a Game" but it didn't FEEL very fun to you. And maybe you didn't enjoy the look of what was supposed to be the prize.

But what if, just maybe, LIFE is indeed a game that we have agreed to play with ourselves. Only to make it more interesting we chose to "forget the rules" and we also "forgot" what the TRUE PRIZE of the game can be?

Every time we WANT something that we don't yet HAVE, in order to ATTRACT it into our world, we must CHANGE who we are BEING.

That's the prize!

Did you miss it?

The prize is the GROWTH; the power, the peace, the skills, the confidence, the feeling EVEN BETTER....BEFORE the "thing" arrives. Then when we get what we want, we can REALLY, REALLY ENJOY it; eyes open, to the power inside ourselves that brought it to us. That's the prize of the game; our power.

Abigail's Story

I SERIOUSLY Want It!

Last Fall I realized I wanted to create something special. I wanted my family to visit my Aunt Nancy in Northern California for the holidays.

My mom and I sat down and looked at what it would cost for us all to visit and it was not in our family budget.

But she didn't want to tell me "no" either. She kept supporting me, saying "maybe there's another way, maybe even a better way for you to get what you really want this holiday".

Together, my mom and I talked to my Aunt Nancy on the phone and did some brainstorming about possibilities; not making any final decisions.

My mom asked me, "what do you really want? What would visiting your Aunt Nancy mean to you"? I said, "I wanted to travel. I wanted to have an adventure. I wanted a different Thanksgiving than we had in the past".

And then an opportunity opened. My Aunt Nancy called me and told me the airlines were running special prices the following month. She asked me if I would be willing to travel alone and spend a whole weekend with her visiting San Francisco city, an aquarium, and a local wildlife area.

I had to think about it. But after some thought, I realized that this would meet all my wishes for travel, adventure, time with family, and something different.

Let's Play a Game Process

Cut out the pieces below or gather your own pieces (buttons, figurines, etc.) from around your house. Place them on the "board"...

Have a good day. Start here.

Good thoughts power you forward.
Worry thoughts, you're stuck here all day.

Problem or challenge
provides opportunity to experiment.
React with fear, fall back one space.
Respond with curiosity, move ahead one
space easily.

Tasks, homework or responsibilities;
smile and move ahead one space.
Complain move back two spaces.

Take a moment to notice
what is going right, what you like
about the day. Remind yourself
what you want today to be about.
Feel good and move ahead one space.

Get some fresh air and exercise.
Remember to smell the flowers,
hear the birds. Feel good and move
ahead one space.

Be really nice
to yourself. Say at least
three nice things to yourself
in your mind.
Move ahead one space.

Sweet Dreams

Be thankful for at least
three things today.
Move ahead one space.

Make someone else's day.
Notice something you like about
someone and let them know
you appreciate them.
Move ahead one space.

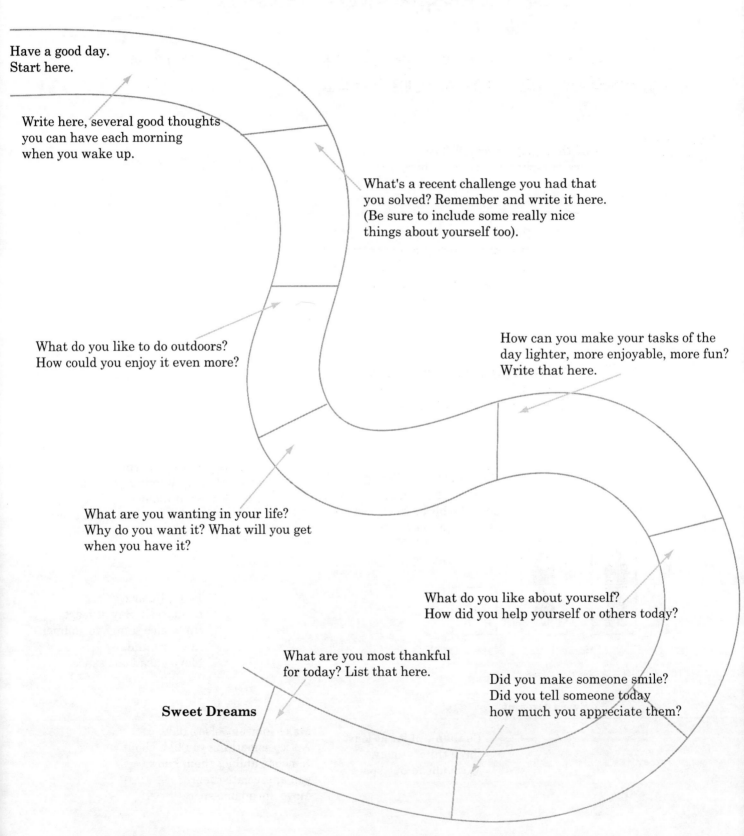

Chapter 4

Your Traveling Companions

Within us we have many "voices" speaking our thoughts to us throughout the day. Most people never notice these voices but they sure follow their directions even if they don't realize it.

Start paying attention to your thoughts. If you don't like what you are hearing, you can change the messages you entertain.

Inside each of us we have two different voices that can be of great value when we pay attention and use their guidance.

One is our intuitive voice. Some people call it the voice of their Angel. Some people call it a "gut feeling". Some people call it the "still quiet voice within". Its purpose is to guide us; always in the direction of our highest good. True intuition always speaks from love and care.

The other is the ego voice. Some people call this their "gremlin". Its job is to keep your physical body safe. Without the ego, or our "beastie", as Abigail likes to call it; we might put our hand on a hot stove over and over, forgetting that it hurt the last time. The ego will use feelings of fear and doubt to keep you away from what it thinks are dangerous situations. It often argues with you and itself, back and forth in your mind.

The ego can mistake any new situation for a danger and flood you with fear or doubt so that you take no risk. This can be quite handy if you are contemplating attempting flight off your roof (don't you try that...) but not so helpful when you want to do your best in front of an audience.

Read on to see how Abigail conquered her fears, stepping into a new experience....

Abigail's Story

I CAN Fly!

The night before my trip up North, I was feeling nervous and my "beastie" was "barking like crazy"! I couldn't sleep. I couldn't even hear my angel.

My mom helped me get to sleep. She had me close my eyes and imagine that I had gone camping overnight with my Aunt Nancy in the past. Together, we imagined all the ways that Aunt Nancy and I had fun, how good it felt, and how I arrived safely back at home three days later from camping.

Even though it was a "pretend" memory; my mom made the whole thing up, it still helped me feel better.

And I had the time of my life in Oakland!

Get to Know YOUR Beauty and Your Beastie

Close your eyes for a moment and listen to the thoughts playing through your mind. Write some of those thoughts here:

_____

_____

_____

If this "voice" had a body or a face, what would it look like? Draw that here:

If you were to give this voice a name, what would that name be? Write that here:

_____

Now close your eyes again for a moment. Place your hand on your heart. Listen inward to hear that still, quiet voice; your inner voice. Does it have anything to say to you? Write that here:

_____

_____

_____

If the message you hear is one of love, that is your Intuitive Voice. That voice guides you toward more love, truth, peace and there is no feeling of doubt or argument.

Your Beastie voice on the other hand, will talk to you about all kinds of things, often one against the other; whatever will keep you thinking the same thoughts over and over so you don't change.

But you can quiet the "yapping" of your "beastie" the same way you win over a frightened dog with kindness. Firmly call your "Beastie" by its name and let it know that you are the one leading the walk and that you want it to come along with you but that you are the master. Just as a kind master, care for your body well; keep it safe and physically fit. Keep speaking calmly and reassuringly to your "beastie" and talk to it about how wonderful life will be when you reach your destination. It will stop it's snarling and barking, and instead help you race along on your journey to a better life!

Chapter 5

We All Live in a Box

Did you know you live in a box; a box made of invisible walls that surround you and keep you living life the same way you did the day before?

So you want stuff but you can't have it yet because it belongs in a bigger box. You can't have anything that "belongs" in a bigger box, without stepping out of the box you are now living in.

That doesn't sound hard; to step out of the box, does it?

But your BEASTIE likes those nice safe walls and it doesn't want you to step outside into the freedom and unknown between boxes. It will say and do almost ANYTHING to keep you where you are!

Abigail's Story

I Want It But I Don't Have It...Yet!

The first time I held a parolette at a local bird store, I couldn't stop thinking about it. Imagine a parrot in a tiny, brilliant green and blue body, small enough to sit in the very palm of your hand. Man, was that cute!

I couldn't stop talking about it either. But I didn't want to just talk about it. I wanted to take one home. At that time, I did not have enough savings to buy a parolette.

I wanted to be a person who took home a parolette. But I wasn't that person yet.

Take a Look Into Your Box

Take a moment and remember what lives in your box; your family, your pets, your room, your school, your friends, even the way you walk home each day. Can you see that in order to have something new, you'll need a "bigger box"?

Write or draw what is in your box now:

```
┌─────────────────────────────────────────┐
│                                         │
│                                         │
│                                         │
│                                         │
│                                         │
└─────────────────────────────────────────┘
```

Now write down what you would like. How much bigger a box will it take to house the new "thing" you are wanting? Draw that new box with the new "thing" in it. Make sure you draw a box big enough for that "new thing" to live in.

Are you ready to live that "bigger life" in that "bigger box" so that "new thing" has a place to live?

PART TWO

THE CREATING PROCESS

The Creating Process

Now you have an understanding of where you need to begin to Make More Good Stuff Happen.

And you might even have a better understanding of why it seemed hard or even impossible in the past.

So how do you step out of your box, build a new box and attract what you now want to live inside?

That's what this next part is all about.

Chapter 6

Why Do You Want It?

Until you can take out your magnifying glass and really get CLEAR about WHY you want something, it's like you don't really mean it.

When you know WHY you want something good, you engage your mind, heart, body and desire to BE, and to do whatever it takes to create a home for that thing or experience to arrive.

Abigail's Story

I Begin!

My mother finally asked me, "why do you want a parolette"?

"I want a companion who can sit on my shoulder and eat off my plate"? I know, it might seem a silly reason to you, but haven't you ever wanted a little friend?

I wanted a little friend that could be with me on my shoulder that could go wherever I went but I didn't have to hold.

I wanted something cute and beautiful, at the same time, that I could enjoy being with.

My mother asked me if I would be willing to explore my options with the goal being that of getting something cute, beautiful, and good company?

I agreed...but I really wanted that parolette!

I want it Because...

Dear Angel:

I want (1) _____(a Pony)

because (2) _____(I want something beautiful and my size)

I want (2) _____ (Something beautiful and my size)

because (3) _____ (I want something that is mine and loves me)

I want (3) _____(Something that is mine and loves me)

because (4) _____ (I want to feel loved by something beautiful)

I want (4) _____ (to feel loved by something beautiful)

because _____ (I want to feel love and see beauty in my life)

Each time you uncover a deeper "why", you strengthen your power to follow through to allow and achieve it.

In our example (in grey) we've discovered, that the desire for a "Pony" is really a desire for "love and beauty". If there was a way to enjoy more "love and beauty" before the "Pony" materialized, you think the enjoyment of that Pony might be even greater? Or perhaps realizing what you really wanted, meant you no longer needed to "chase after" a Pony?

See Me, Hear Me

Stand in front of a mirror alone, smile and tell yourself about what you want and why you want it.

Go ahead, let it all out. Really put some FEELING into it.

Why do you want this "thing"?

Chapter 7

Believing is Seeing

The world says it backwards, Seeing isn't believing; BELIEVING is SEEING.

You won't see anything without the willingness to believe it is possible first.

You don't have to believe it all at once. You can start with little bits and create a stronger and stronger belief.

Watch and listen carefully, and your Angel will bring you little encouraging signs to strengthen your belief that what you want is on its way.

Abigail's Story

Making it Real!

I started making my goal seem real to me by searching the internet for articles about, and photos of, parolettes. I checked out books from the library. I began to research how much a bird, the cage, and the food would cost so I knew just how much to start saving.

Whenever we were near the bird shop, I asked to go in and visit with the staff. I asked them lots of questions.

It still felt big, but not impossible.

Treasure Map

Get a large piece of paper, something just the right size for you to play with, that feels good in front of you on the table. Now gather a bunch of old magazines (sometimes libraries sell old magazines for a dime) and begin looking through the pictures. Tear or cut out pictures to create a collage of all the images that remind you of that "thing" that you are wanting or how that "thing" would make you feel (happy, excited, pleased, energized). Cut out words from the magazines that describe feelings you associate with that "thing".

Your treasure map might show a pool with the words "cool", "refreshing", "relax", "fun". Or maybe you have pictures of friends playing and pets fetching toys with words like "friendship", "love", "baseball", "beach". You get the idea.

Put your treasure map where you can see it before you go to sleep at night and the moment you wake up so that images of what you want are the last thing you see before you sleep and the first thing you see when you wake.

Chapter 8

BE DO HAVE

Most people think you have to "have" the tool to "do" the action to "be" the one who has accomplished the task, achieved the goal, or received the goods.

But as we explored before, what actually happens is that before anything gets DONE, you have to make a decision, a BEING choice that "starts your engine and takes your foot off the brake" so that you can "drive the car" and "get where you want to go".

You must decide to BE the person who follows through to the ACTION to earn and attract THE THING.

So what if you want to visit the Grand Canyon and you don't have a car? If you decide to BE the person who'll DO whatever it takes (safely) to HAVE the trip, what then?

That's what we're going to explore in our next chapter.

Abigail's Story

I'm the Person Who Never Gives Up!

Weeks went by, and then a month. But I didn't stop talking about my parolette. I kept thinking about it. I kept reading about parrots and other types of birds.

I asked my mother daily for paid chores. I asked my neighbors for work. No amount of work was too small. I kept collecting savings. I counted my money saved, every day, sometimes several times a day.

I began leaving my money at home so I wouldn't be tempted. I did make some purchases, but I passed others by, choosing to save.

Everyday I felt like I was getting a bit closer.

My Personal Scene

Take out a piece of paper. For extra dramatic effect, decorate it anyway that feels good.

Now, think of what you want (that thing, or experience). Write it's name at the top of the paper. Imagine you already had it. Really play with all your inner senses for a moment.

What do you look like in that imagination? Are there other people with you? Are you smiling? Are you moving or still? Does it feel good to have that thing, or be in that experience?

Write about your experience as if it were happening to you right now. Or draw a picture of what it looks like to be "in your own scene".

If it feels better, stand up and move around just the way you do in your "inner scene". Pretend that you are that person now.

The more often you can PRACTICE living in "your own scene" of what you want, the more clear you will become about WHO you must be and become, and what feels good to do as a next step, to attract that thing of experience into your every-day-world.

Chapter 9

Magnetic Formula For Momentum

Left to its own devices, the ego mind, our "beastie", will choose to focus on why we don't have something or why we can't have something. This does not help us move forward toward what we desire. And it builds a wall that repels our desire away from us!

What to do then if we really, really do want that "thing" or "experience"? Well, we have to recognize that we have both a "beastie" and an "angel" voice. Both are powerful.

To get them both working FOR us...we have to take charge and share with them our picture of what we are wanting.

If you go into a restaurant and order potatoes, what will you expect to receive; French Fries, mashed, or a 5 pound sack?

Without a clear order, the waitress is left to guess. She might bring you mashed potatoes and ask, "is this what you wanted"?

That's what happens when we get something back that is NOT that "thing" or "experience" that we have identified as something we are wanting. It's just the Universe's way of asking, "is this what you meant"?

It doesn't mean your process isn't working. It's just feedback. Take note. Say "thank you for the response". And "let me be a bit more clear". You might want to repeat the following process (page 44) to create attraction and motion.

When you realize the waitress needs more information, then you can say, "I'd like curly French Fries, with extra spice and Ranch dressing on the side". Now the waitress is much more clear about what it is you are wanting. And it is easier and faster for her to deliver it to you.

Abigail's Story

Setting "Magnetic Forces" in Motion!

One afternoon, during a car ride home, my mother helped me work through the "magnetizing process".

Here's what my "Magnetizing Process" looked like:

What is it you are wanting to create?

My own parolette bird

What is one part of that "thing" or "experience" that you can focus on magnetizing first?

The money to buy my bird

Why do you want that "thing" or "experience"? (Make it good!)

I want a pet that I can hold in my hand and will sit on my shoulder. I want to buy it on my own, with my own money.

Pretend you were someone who already had that "thing" or "experience". What would you see around you?

I see myself collecting allowance, and working for the neighbors. I see myself saving the money in a jar with a picture of a bird taped on the front. I see myself putting the money in my wallet. I see myself handing the woman at the bird store the money out of my wallet. I see a brightly colored bird, with tiny eyes, hopping from my hand to my shoulder. I see myself holding the bird in a cage on my lap in the car.

What would you hear around you?

I hear the coins dropping into the jar. I hear my mother calling me to get into the car. I hear the loud bird calls of the bird store. I hear my brother say he wishes he had a bird too. I hear my bird scrambling around in her cage.

What thoughts would be going through your mind?

Wow, that wasn't as hard as I thought! I did this on my own. I could do it again. I can't wait to show my bird it's new home.

What feelings would you feel in your heart?

I'm excited, excited, excited. I can't wait to get to the store and get my bird!

What would your body feel like?

Like dancing!

What would you be doing?

I'm counting my money and organizing it so I'm ready to go get my bird.

Who would you ask to support you and what would you ask them to help you with?

Mom, do you know of any work I can do for money? Do you have any chores that you will pay me for?

Now it's your turn....

Magnetizing Process

What is it you are wanting to create? _____

_____

What is one part of that "thing" or "experience" that you can focus on magnetizing first? _____

_____

Why do you want that "thing" or "experience"? (Make it good!) _____

_____

Pretend you were someone who already had that "thing" or "experience". What would you see around you? _____

_____

_____

What would you hear around you? _____

_____

What thoughts would be going through your mind?

_____

_____

What feelings would you feel in your heart? _____

_____

_____

What would your body feel like?

_____

_____

_____

What would you be doing? _____

_____

_____

Who would you ask to support you and what would you ask them to help you with? _____

_____

Chapter 10

First Believe Then Take Action

Is your belief stronger, now that you have worked through your magnetizing process, that you CAN have what you want?

Can you FEEL how it is possible to begin moving closer to that "thing" or "experience" as it is drawn closer to you?

Great!

Now, this next part is the part, that many people do not understand. And this next part is the part where many people stumble, and lose their way.

In order to BE the one who can "allow", "accept" and "receive" the "thing" or "experience", you MUST take a step toward it first, then those "magnetic forces" (remember the Law of Attraction) come into play and pull that "thing" or "experience" toward you just as strongly.

You must take some action. Or it's like placing an order and then leaving the restaurant. You never really meant to "receive" that "order".

When you take an action, it fuels your confidence, sense of deserving, and belief in yourself.

If you don't take action, chances are you have NOT truly chosen to BE the person to accept the "thing" or "experience".

When you really FEEL your choice to BE the person to accept the "thing" or "experience", taking some action, no matter how small, will be something you feel moved to do. You'll WANT to take action.

Abigail's Story

In the Meantime!

While waiting for the money to materialize to buy my bird, I started studying other birds. I held other birds at the store. I got different opinions from the staff about the best bird for me.

I went back and did some research on the temperaments, life span, playfulness, and other qualities of several other types of birds; parakeet, cockatiel, and senegal parrot.

I researched costs involved and compared. I looked for people who had these other birds and asked them for their stories.

Maybe there was a bird that was a better match for me and still fit the qualities I was looking for and my budget.

Not all Actions are Alike

Which action do you think or feel might be more effective, might bring that "thing" or "experience" to you more swiftly?

Would it be an action you didn't really want to do but everyone told you was the thing to do?

Or would it be an action you felt really excited about, good about doing?

Hey, we could be on to something here. Not all actions are alike. What "works" for one person works because of the way they "FEEL" about their action.

So let's find an action that takes us closer to what we are wanting that we can ENJOY doing.

What do you want? _____

Sit quietly alone and place your hands gently on your forehead. Ask your mind, "what is an action I could take, one that I could take today, that I can feel good about, and that moves me closer to what I am wanting"? What does your mind's voice tell you? _____

_____

Now place your hands gently over your heart. Ask your heart, "what is an action I could take, one that I could take today, that I can feel good about, and that moves me closer to what I am wanting"? What does your heart's voice tell you? _____

_____

Now rest your hands comfortably, open palm. Ask your Soul, "what is an action I could take, one that I could take today, that I can feel good about, and that moves me closer to what I am wanting"? What does your soul's voice tell you?

_____

_____

Check in with your Angel and your Beastie. What do each of them have to say? Will your Ego-mind or Beastie agree to work with you to complete this action?

_____

_____

Now that the whole group has given some input, what feels good, do-able, the next step, specially designed, FOR YOU, BY YOU? Write that action here.

_____

_____

Now take action! And celebrate when you're done. Say to yourself, "all right, I did it, I'm someone who is moving toward my goals and what I want is on its way to me"! (It's even better if you can jump for joy or high-five yourself, or give yourself a hug and a "way to go"!) _____

Chapter 11

The Gap

Creating what you are wanting in your life can take just a moment or it may take some substantial time.

You could call this "the gap" between what you are experiencing right now, and what you want to experience more.

Remember when you last planted a seed? It seemed to take forever to come up and even longer before you were able to eat the ripe fruit. That's just how long it took.

The Gap is a place where many people choose to become "discouraged". But it can also be a very important place to take the time to experiment, magnetize something EVEN BETTER than what you are wanting to have or experience, and maybe most important; a place where you are free to change your mind.

Imagine if every wish came true in a flash! You might not want it that way. When was the last time you had a nightmare or had a thought of something you were afraid of? With "instant creation" you might find a lot more monsters running loose. Would you REALLY want your thoughts to instantly take form?

I don't think so. So the next time you feel tense or frustrated because you think it's taking too long for your dreams to come into being, you could stop and instead remember that "the gap" is where you have the freedom to rechoose or change your mind.

Yes, sometimes it takes a bit longer for your dream to arrive. Your patience and an attitude of joyful anticipation, allows the power of the entire Universe to work on your behalf to bring you something EVEN BETTER than you had asked for. Cool!

And when you practice the skills in this book, you get to "live your dream" every day, you don't have to wait to feel all the feelings of that "thing" or "experience".

Abigail's Story

The Waiting!

I honestly can't remember how I survived the long wait. I think maybe part of it was that I began having doubts about the parolette because they liked to nip and I wanted something gentle and friendly.

So I used the waiting time to look around for other options.

My mom helped keep me focused by asking me questions that helped me keep going and encouraged me.

Looking for Clues

While you are waiting for your dream to take form, you can strengthen your belief, leave the door open for new opportunities and an even better experience as you move forward in time to it's creation. You can do this by looking for, and making notes of, clues that it is on it's way.

Put on your detective clothes and grab your magnifying glass and go looking for the clues that can tell you that what you are wanting is on it's way.

Below, write down any clue that might tell you or show you that what you are wanting is coming your way:

_____

_____

_____

_____

_____

_____

Clues might include: dreams about what you want, other people talking about what you want, things you see that remind you of what you want, opportunities to work or visit with someone who already has what you want, new ideas about how to get closer to what you want, even more thoughts about what you want.

Chapter 12

How Do You Know When It's Working?

Picture a vegetable garden where all you see is a cleared space of good earth. First you plant the seeds. Does anything "look" like something is happening yet?

Probably not. But you know what you want; juicy, red tomatoes. So you water every day.

What happens next? Probably, even before the tomato seeds start to emerge you see something else; weeds sprouting!

But the weeds tell you something. They're a clue (like we talked about in the last chapter). They tell you the ground is fertile and the water is nurturing your desire for ripe tomatoes.

So you take care of weeding the garden, right? And you keep watering, knowing the seeds were true.

What would happen if about now, you grew impatient and dug up the seeds to see if they were growing? Right, you'd destroy the forming plants.

Finally, the seeds sprout and your tiny tomato plants begin to emerge. Do you get to eat the ripe tomatoes tonight? Not yet.

Can you speed up the tomatoes growth? You bet. If you water, and mulch, and fertilize, and stake and care for them well each day, they will grow and form much more quickly and easily than in a yard left to struggle against weeds, drought and stray animals.

And still, you get the ripe tomatoes when you get the ripe tomatoes. You can choose to eat them before they are ripe, or you can choose to care for them until they are just what you imagined.

It's no different with your "magnetizing process".

You realize you want some "thing" or "experience" and you set it's forming in motion with a strong, clear, true seed-thought and new BEING choice (you must choose to be the gardener).

The first thing to pop up are the weeds; the negative thoughts and blocks to having what you are wanting to create. Do not let these weeds choke your garden.

One of three things can happen that will tell you your magnetic process is working:

1. The "weeds will come up"; those negative thoughts and habits that will choke your garden if you let them. You must choose to be the gardener and take each negative thought out of your garden; water your garden with the positive thoughts and actions that will nurture it.

2. You will begin to see the sprouting seeds and continued growth of your seed-thought. But look carefully so you do not squash one of your new plants, or dig them up by not recognizing and appreciating their growth.

3. New opportunities and synchronicities will appear for you to exercise your power of choice. This is where you get to choose to eat "green tomatoes" or wait until they are "ripe".

These can happen separately, in combination and at anytime during the process. They are all signs that your garden is growing toward ripe fruit. So how then shall you tend your garden?

One final "gardening tip". When you experience doubt, or worry; and allow those to disturb your faith in your success; well, that's just like digging up your tender little seedlings and having to start all over again. Care for your growing desires as if they were precious growing seedlings that need care and support and you will be rewarded when their growing cycle has reached the fruit stage.

Abigail's Story

When I Knew I Was Making Progress!

One afternoon, we stopped at the bird store. I had my wallet with $125 dollars in it. There on the counter stood a cage with the sweetest, liveliest little birds; hand-tamed zebra finches.

Oh man, I flipped for one of those little birds. It was light as a feather on my finger and it hopped onto my shoulder and back. And guess what, including the cage and food it was...you guessed it; almost exactly $125.

As we rode home in the car, I held my bird in it's little box on my lap and I felt like dancing; just like in my magnetizing process.

It had all come together in right timing, even better than I had imagined. My little bird has been a great joy for me and never nipped me even once. She sits on my finger and flies to my shoulder. She hops around the table as I do my homework.

It's Working

What do you want? _____

What are you experiencing now? _____

_____

Is that a "weed"? _____

If so, what is a another thought or feeling or action you could have or do that feels better and "weeds the garden"? _____

_____

Is it a clue that you are magnetizing what you want? _____

If so, what can you do to celebrate the new growth in your garden? _____

_____

Is it an opportunity to say "yes" or "no, thank you" to help make your choice more "real?

_____

What next? _____

Chapter 13

The Power Pause

Would you like a special, "magic wand" that could "soothe" the Beastie's grumblings and invite the Angel to sing as you "super-powered" your way through watering and weeding and celebrating your "garden's growth"?

Here's an amazing, simple and fun way to increase the power of your "magnet" and "magnetizing" what you are wanting to create, that works "like magic".

It's called the Power Pause and if you want more information just visit www.richbits.com or contact us ("how to" on last page of the book).

Using the Power Pause you can "leap over every wall", "avoid any pitfall" and send a very clear "order" to the Universe for what you are wanting and how you want to experience it.

Here are the super simple steps of the Power Pause:

1. Go to a place of peace, either in your mind or in your home and FEEL that peace. You might like to watch, listen to, or feel your breath flowing in and out. You might like to imagine in your mind a beautiful place and imagine you were there until you feel really good and relaxed.

2. Imagine or pretend in your mind and heart that you are now in the setting that includes all the pieces of what you are wanting to experience. If you want a pool, pretend you feel the cool water on your skin, hear the splashes of friends near you, see the reflections of the water moving back and forth.

Make that pretend experience as real as possible. Smell the smells, feel the feelings. BE in that experience as if it is happening to you right now. ENJOY it right now.

3. Place your hand over your heart and feel how much you appreciate being in that experience; having that thing, being with those people, doing those activities. Say aloud or to yourself, "thank you, thank you so much". You may say "thank you God" or "thank you Creator", Use a name for the "Highest Power" that fits for you.

Abigail's Story

I Can Practice Having It Everyday!

My mom taught me that I don't have to wait to have something.

Everyday I can relax, imagine having it, feel how good it feels to have it as if I were enjoying it right now, and say "thank you" that it's on its way.

When she told me I could use the Power Pause to help me bring anything into my life that I wanted, the first thing I thought of was a beautiful pool in our own backyard.

The More you Power Pause, the Better

The Power Pause can last from a minute to an hour. Most people take about 1-3 minutes to practice the Power Pause.

Use the Power Pause:

- When you aren't feeling so good, when you're feeling discouraged or negative thoughts are running through your mind.

- To talk to your Beastie and Angel, to let them know where you want to go as a team.

- To feel even better when you feel good, or to celebrate your accomplishments.

- Whenever fear or doubt start circling and threatening.

- To pluck those "weeds" and super-nourish your garden.

- Everyday, even when you're feeling great and then it becomes a habit that automatically "kicks in" to quiet fear or doubt.

Chapter 14

Powerpacts

When we get together with others who want us to succeed and we support them too, we all are more powerful.

Isn't it easier to accomplish ANYTHING when we know others believe in, and support, us? And doesn't it feel good to tell someone we know they "can do it" and mean it?

Share your dream or goal only with those you know can see it, and feel it for you and with you; who believe in you and your power. This will strengthen you.

And be a supportive, believing friend for others and their dreams. When you see your friends' dreams coming true, you are actually helping them be more powerful magnets for what they want...and your magnet is stronger too!

Abigail's Story

I Believe It, She Believes It, I Know It's Coming True!

I think that one of the reasons I got my bird was that I kept talking to everyone who would listen and tell me I could have what I wanted.

I talked to teachers, librarians, bird technicians, my family, my friends, neighbors, my dentist...even my dog!

Each of those people helped me achieve what I wanted by seeing it with me, and for me. (I wonder what the picture of my bird looked like in my dog's head?)

Create Your Own Powerpact

"Powerpact" is the term Darel Rutherford gives for a very special gathering. This gathering can happen in person, on the phone, even by mail.

The most important part of this gathering is that each person gathering follows this one purpose; to believe and support the others, to listen to their dreams and desires, to act as a mirror that shines back confidence, and believe in the power and brilliance of the others in the gathering.

In this "Powerpact" each member feels better about himself or herself because they know they have confidence in the others, and the others have confidence in him or her.

Talk about magic! Amazing things occur to those who take the time, energy and focus to meet regularly with one, or two others to listen and share successes, dreams and desires.

Who do you know that you would like to support by meeting regularly (once a week works well) to listen to their dreams and share your own?

Take the next step and talk to them. Perhaps they would be delighted to meet and share in this deep and loving way.

Chapter 15

Gratitude

And so we end where we began; with gratitude, and yet it is just the beginning again.

When you begin and end the desire for some "thing" or some "experience" with gratitude, you attract people, things and situations to be grateful for, and about, the whole way through the process.

Darel likes to say that "Gratitude is the most powerful prayer on the planet" and I'll agree.

When you express your celebration for what you receive and your thankfulness for the clues and arrival of that "thing" or "experience" that you have been wanting to create in your life; it's like saying yes to the Universe and your magnet gets bigger, your process gets faster, and you get what you are wanting more easily and quickly.

Practice gratitude about everything and watch how the positive results in your life soar!

Abigail's Story

Thank You for my Wonderful Bird!

One of the best things about getting my bird was that my friend, Brinn was with me when I brought her home. Together we celebrated getting what I wanted.

I did feel very thankful that day and for a long time after about my new bird. I couldn't wipe the smile off my face for days. Even now, when I think about it, I smile. And a smile is a wonderful "thank you".

An Attitude of Gratitude

What are you grateful for right now? What do you want to say "thank you" for? What do you appreciate? Write those here:

_____

_____

_____

_____

What could you be grateful for? Be grateful for that as if it were here now and write "thank you" for those "things" or "experiences" below:

_____

_____

_____

_____

Chapter 16

What Now?

Start with something you want. Make it real enough you can almost believe it, but far enough away that it's going to take some attention, and not so far that you can't possibly believe it.

Now go back to chapter one, and play, play, PLAY your way through the book again!

Contacting us.....
Thank you for purchasing

How To Make More Good Stuff Happen

We welcome your correspondence.
You may reach us at Deb@richbits.com or DAR Publishing, darel@richbits.com.

Deborah Ivanoff is a Certified Master Being Coach
She coaches clients one-on-one and
co-hosts with Darel Rutherford
16-week BEING THE SOLUTION and 6-month
MASTERING YOUR LIFE transformational workshops.

Abigail Ivanoff-Achenbach is an active "tween", avid reader, animal advocate, vegetarian and loyal friend.

For more information visit www.richbits.com or
e-mail directly Deb@richbits.com

Notes